W9-DGF-652

GRAPHIC NONFICTION

RICHARD the LIONHEART

THE LIFE OF A KING AND CRUSADER

by
DAVID WEST & JACKIE GAFF

illustrated by
JOHN COOPER

The Rosen Publishing Group, Inc., New York

Published in 2005 by The Rosen Publishing Group, Inc.
29 East 21st Street, New York, NY 10010

Designed and produced by
David West Books

Editor: Gail Bushnell
Photo Research: Carlotta Cooper

Photo credits:
Pages 4, 45 (top) – Rex Features Ltd.
Pages 6 (both), 7, 44, 44–45 – Mary Evans Picture Library
Page 45 – The Culture Archive

Library of Congress Cataloging-in-Publication Data

West, David, 1956–
    Richard the Lionheart : the life of a king and crusader / by David West & Jackie Gaff. —1st ed.
    p. cm. — (Graphic nonfiction)
    Includes bibliographical references (p.) and index.
    ISBN 1-4042-0241-2 (lib. bdg.)
    1. Richard I, King of England, 1157–1199—Juvenile literature. 2. Great Britain—History—Richard I, 1189–1199—Juvenile literature. 3. Great Britain—Kings and rulers—Biography—Juvenile literature. 4. Crusades—Third, 1189–1192—Juvenile literature. I. Gaff, Jackie. II. Title. III. Series.

    DA207.W46 2005
    942.03'2'092—dc22

                                                                    2004011267

Manufactured in China

CONTENTS

WHO'S WHO

Richard the Lionheart (1157–1199) In 1189, Richard became king of England and also inherited most of northern and western France. In 1190–1192, he went on a crusade to the Holy Land, then under Muslim control.

Henry II (1133–1189) Richard's father, Henry, married Eleanor of Aquitaine in 1152 and became king of England in 1154.

Eleanor of Aquitaine (1122–1204) Richard's mother, Eleanor, inherited much of western France on her father's death in 1137. Control of these lands passed to her husband, Henry, when they married.

Henry the Younger (1155–1183) Richard's older brother, and the heir to the throne of England until his death.

Philip II (1165–1223) King of France from 1180, Philip wanted control of Henry II's French lands. He plotted first with Richard and his brothers against their father, and then later against Richard.

Saladin (1137–1193) After becoming ruler of Egypt and Syria in the early 1170s, Saladin led his Muslim army in a war against the Christians in the Holy Land.

THE ANGEVIN EMPIRE

When his father, Henry II, died in 1189, Richard the Lionheart inherited the kingdom of England along with most of northern and western France. Henry II's family name was Angevin. The family's vast lands were called the Angevin Empire.

FEUDAL KINGDOMS

In those days, Western Europe was governed by a system known as feudalism. Under feudalism the king owned all the land in his kingdom. He granted land to his nobles for them to live on. In return, the nobles paid homage – a promise to be loyal to their king and to supply knights to fight for him during times of war. The promise to fight for your king was important, as rulers were always going to war. They fought to defend their lands from attackers and to put down rebellions by powerful nobles. They also fought to win new lands from other rulers.

HOLDING THE FORT

A castle was the key to defending the land around it. If a castle was taken, so was its land. In Angevin times, armies rarely fought large battles. Instead, all their efforts usually went into capturing castles. ⬇

FAMILY TREE
This chart shows the children of Henry II and Eleanor of Aquitaine. Richard was Eleanor and Henry's third son. Their first son was three when he died. Richard became Henry II's heir on the death of Henry the Younger in 1183.

HENRY II married ELEANOR OF
1133–1189 1152 AQUITAINE
1122–1204

— WILLIAM
1153–1156

— HENRY THE YOUNGER
1155–1183

— MATILDA
1156–1189

— RICHARD I
1157–1199

— GEOFFREY
1158–1186

— ELEANOR
1161–1214

— JOAN
1165–1199

— JOHN
1167–1216

THE LAND OF FRANCE

The Angevin family controlled far more land in France than the French king. But under feudalism, the French king was the Angevins' lord. They were supposed to pay homage to him for their lands in France. In practice, the Angevins were so powerful that they only paid homage to the French king when they wanted to. They treated their lands in France as though it was their own separate kingdom.

KEY TO THE MAP

Maximum extent of Angevin empire under Richard I

Kingdom of France

■ Castle

Nottingham

ENGLAND

Oxford •

London •

Dover •

• Winchester

Portsmouth •

• Boulogne

FLANDERS

ENGLISH CHANNEL

Château-Gaillard ■ ■ Gisors

CHAMPAGNE

NORMANDY

Seine R.

• Paris

Bonmoulins ■ Verneuil

BLOIS

BRITTANY

MAINE

Le Mans •

• Vézelay

ANJOU

Tours

• Blois

BURGUNDY

Saumur ■

Fontevraud •

TOURAINE

■ Chinon

POITOU

■ Châteauroux

• Poitiers

BERRY

AQUITAINE

• Lusignan

LA MARCHE

SAINTONGE

Taillebourg •

Chabanais

Saintes •

ANGOUMOIS

• Limoges

• Angoulême

Chalus

AUVERGNE

LIMOUSIN

PÉRIGORD

HOLY ROMAN EMPIRE

N
W   E
S

AGENAIS

GASCONY

TOULOUSE

• Marseille

NAVARRE

ARAGON

MEN OF WAR

In Richard the Lionheart's time, knights were highly trained warriors who fought on horseback. The chainmail armor and trained warhorse that a knight needed were expensive. As a result, most knights were either the sons of other knights or wealthy noblemen.

THE CODE OF CHIVALRY

As well as being brave and skillful warriors, knights were expected to follow the code of chivalry. This meant behaving with honor at all times toward all people, including your enemies. A chivalrous knight was also supposed to be ready to die in defense of the Christian religion. In reality, though, few knights lived up to this ideal.

THE YOUNG RICHARD

Little is known about Richard's early life. Although he grew up to be an excellent horseman and fearless warrior, nothing is known of his training as a knight. He was born on September 8, 1157, in the English town of Oxford. He probably spent his first years in England. By the time

WEAPONS OF WAR
A knight's chief weapon was a long, heavy spear called a lance. He could also use a sword or a battle-ax. To protect himself, he carried a shield. If he could afford them, he also wore a metal helmet and chainmail armor.

his youngest brother, John, was born ten years later, his parents were growing apart. His mother, Eleanor, was spending more time in Aquitaine than in England. Richard was probably with her.

MILITARY BACKUP
Peasants were rarely asked to go to war for their lord. It was more important to be at home, looking after the land. If knights needed foot soldiers to back them up, they mainly employed mercenaries.

Pilgrims are believers who make a journey called a pilgrimage to a holy place. In Richard's time, people on a pilgrimage carried a long walking stick called a staff and a bag called a scrip.

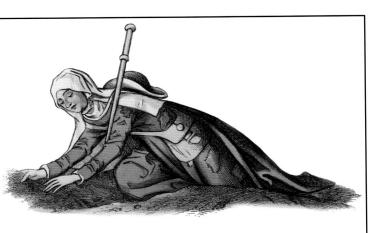

RICHARD THE CRUSADER

One of the greatest adventures of Richard's life was his crusade to the Holy Land in the Middle East in 1190–1192. Crusades were religious wars fought by Christians to win control of Jerusalem and the Holy Land. The wars began in the late eleventh century, after Muslim Turks from central Asia captured Jerusalem. The Muslims then stopped Christian pilgrims from visiting the city. By the time Richard was born, the Holy Land was again a Christian kingdom. In 1187, Jerusalem was recaptured by the army of the Muslim ruler Saladin. As a Christian ruler and a chivalrous knight, Richard believed his duty was to free the Holy Land.

THE HOLY CITY
Jerusalem is a holy place for Jews, Muslims, and Christians. It is holy for Christians because many events in Jesus' life happened there. For Muslims, it is the place from which their prophet Muhammad rose to heaven.

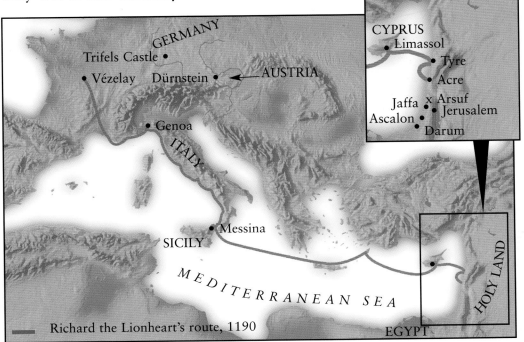

x Battle site

CYPRUS
- Limassol

• Tyre

• Acre

Jaffa • x Arsuf
Ascalon • • Jerusalem
• Darum

GERMANY

Trifels Castle •

• Vézelay Dürnstein • ← AUSTRIA

• Genoa

ITALY

• Messina
SICILY

MEDITERRANEAN SEA

HOLY LAND

—— Richard the Lionheart's route, 1190

EGYPT

RICHARD the LIONHEART
THE LIFE OF A KING AND CRUSADER

DING DONG DING

WHAT'S ALL THE NOISE ABOUT?

WE'VE GOT A NEW DUKE.

IN JUNE 1172, THE BELLS OF THE CITY OF LIMOGES RANG OUT IN CELEBRATION.

LIMOGES WAS AN IMPORTANT CITY IN AQUITAINE, THE LARGEST AND WEALTHIEST REGION IN FRANCE. AQUITAINE HAD BECOME PART OF KING HENRY II OF ENGLAND'S EMPIRE IN 1152, WHEN HE MARRIED ELEANOR, DUCHESS OF AQUITAINE. HENRY INHERITED HIS NORTHERN FRENCH LANDS – NORMANDY, MAINE, ANJOU, AND TOURAINE – FROM HIS PARENTS. HENRY WAS ALSO LORD OF BRITTANY.

NOW, HENRY AND ELEANOR'S SON RICHARD WAS BEING MADE DUKE OF AQUITAINE. HE WAS ONLY 14 YEARS OLD THOUGH. HIS FATHER HELD THE REAL POWER.

I'M GLAD YOU ARE DUKE OF MY LANDS, RICHARD.

IT'S ALL VERY WELL, MOTHER. BUT FATHER **STILL** HOLDS ALL THE POWER.

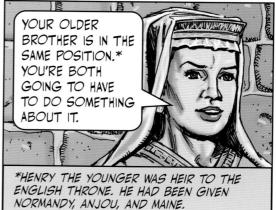

YOUR OLDER BROTHER IS IN THE SAME POSITION.* YOU'RE BOTH GOING TO HAVE TO DO SOMETHING ABOUT IT.

*HENRY THE YOUNGER WAS HEIR TO THE ENGLISH THRONE. HE HAD BEEN GIVEN NORMANDY, ANJOU, AND MAINE.

ELEANOR AND HER HUSBAND WERE NO LONGER CLOSE. SHE ENCOURAGED HENRY THE YOUNGER AND RICHARD TO SIDE WITH HER **AGAINST** HIM. THE FRENCH KING, LOUIS VII, ALSO URGED THE BOYS TO REBEL. HENRY THE YOUNGER WAS MARRIED TO LOUIS'S DAUGHTER, MARGARET, SO THE FRENCH KING WAS HIS FATHER-IN-LAW.

LOUIS, FATHER HAS GIVEN THREE OF **MY** CASTLES TO MY YOUNGEST BROTHER, JOHN.

YOUR FATHER WILL NEVER LET YOU TAKE CONTROL OF YOUR LANDS, HENRY.

HENRY RETURNED TO FACE HIS FATHER...

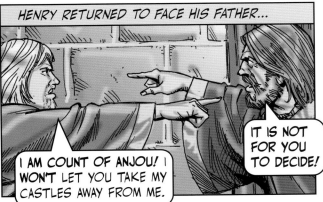

I AM COUNT OF ANJOU! I WON'T LET YOU TAKE MY CASTLES AWAY FROM ME.

IT IS NOT FOR YOU TO DECIDE!

THEN HAND OVER POWER TO ME IN SOME OF MY LANDS.

YOU MIGHT BE 18, BUT YOU'RE **NOT YET** READY TO RULE!

THE TWO HENRYS QUARRELED EVERY TIME THEY MET.

BUT WORSE WAS TO COME. A TERRIBLE RUMOR REACHED KING HENRY IN LIMOGES.

YOUR WIFE AND SONS ARE NOW PLOTTING AGAINST YOU.

KING HENRY LEFT THE CITY IN A HURRY. HE TOOK HIS ELDEST SON, HENRY, WITH HIM. THE KING SAID HE WAS GOING HUNTING, BUT HIS ORDERS TO HIS MEN SHOWED THAT HE WAS TAKING NO CHANCES...

MAKE THE CASTLE READY FOR WAR.

ONE NIGHT, HENRY THE YOUNGER **ESCAPED**. HE HEADED FOR THE COURT OF HIS FATHER-IN-LAW, LOUIS VII IN PARIS.

ELEANOR SENT RICHARD AND HIS BROTHER GEOFFREY TO PARIS.* THEN SHE CALLED HER NOBLES TO REBEL AGAINST HER HUSBAND.

CALL THE MEN TO ARMS!

*GEOFFREY WAS A YEAR YOUNGER THAN RICHARD.

IN SPRING 1173, RICHARD WAS KNIGHTED BY LOUIS VII. ALL THREE BROTHERS SWORE HIM AN OATH NOT TO MAKE PEACE WITH THEIR FATHER.

MANY POWERFUL MEN JOINED FORCES WITH ELEANOR AND LOUIS VII AS THEY PREPARED TO GO TO WAR AGAINST KING HENRY. AMONG THEIR ALLIES WERE MANY OF LOUIS'S NOBLES.

KING HENRY WAS ONE OF THE WEALTHIEST MEN IN EUROPE. WHEN THE WAR BROKE OUT IN JULY 1173, HE WAS **READY**. HE HAD USED HIS FUNDS TO EMPLOY MERCENARIES.

RICHARD AND HIS BROTHERS TOOK PART IN AN ATTACK ON NORMANDY. BUT THE INVASION DID NOT LAST LONG AND WAS SOON CALLED OFF.

OTHER ATTACKS AGAINST KING HENRY WERE ALSO SHORT-LIVED. IN THE FALL, HE OFFERED PEACE TERMS TO HIS SONS AND LOUIS VII. LOUIS ADVISED THE BROTHERS TO TURN THEM DOWN.

YOUR FATHER OFFERS **MONEY**, NOT POWER.

KING HENRY BEGAN A NEW ATTACK AGAINST THE REBELS' CASTLES IN TOURAINE.

ELEANOR WAS FORCED TO FLEE...

THIS SQUIRE'S CLOTHES SHOULD FIT.

QUICK! THE KING'S MEN ARE COMING.

HALT! SEARCH THE WAGON.

WHAT HAVE WE GOT HERE?

TAKE YOUR HANDS OFF ME!

ELEANOR WAS TAKEN TO KING HENRY AS A PRISONER.

RICHARD TOOK OVER LEADERSHIP OF ELEANOR'S REBEL NOBLES.

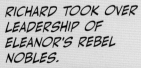

WE MUST FIGHT ON AND FREE MY MOTHER.

BUT KING HENRY WAS WINNING. IN JULY 1174, HE BEGAN PEACE TALKS WITH HIS SON HENRY AND LOUIS VII OF FRANCE. RICHARD FELT BETRAYED.

MY FRIENDS HAVE **TURNED** ON ME!

RICHARD GAVE UP A FEW WEEKS LATER. HE THREW HIMSELF AT HIS FATHER'S FEET...

LET US MAKE THE KISS OF PEACE.

FORGIVE ME, FATHER.

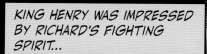

KING HENRY WAS IMPRESSED BY RICHARD'S FIGHTING SPIRIT...

TAKE CONTROL OF MY ARMY IN AQUITAINE. SMASH THE REBELS' CASTLES TO PIECES!

TO MAKE SURE ALL HIS SONS REMAINED LOYAL, THE KING KEPT ELEANOR CAPTIVE IN ENGLAND.

PEACE WAS NOT WON EASILY IN AQUITAINE. BY SPRING 1176, RICHARD FOUND HIMSELF UP AGAINST A NEW GROUP OF REBELS. THIS NEW REBEL GROUP WAS TOO STRONG FOR RICHARD TO DEFEAT WITHOUT HELP. HE WENT TO ENGLAND TO SEE HIS FATHER.

IN APRIL, RICHARD RETURNED TO AQUITAINE WITH MONEY TO HIRE MERCENARIES.

MY LORD, THE BAD NEWS IS THAT YOUR ENEMIES HAVE **ALSO** EMPLOYED MERCENARIES.

RICHARD DEFEATED THE REBELS' MERCENARY ARMY IN MAY. BUT THE WIN DID NOT PUT AN END TO THE REBELLION.

HENRY THE YOUNGER JOINED RICHARD FOR A SHORT TIME...

FATHER HAS SENT ME, BUT I'VE HAD **ENOUGH** OF WAR. I WANT TO GO ON A PILGRIMAGE.

FORTUNATELY, RICHARD HAD ALREADY CAPTURED KEY REBEL CASTLES. NOW HE LAID SIEGE TO ANGOULÊME. MOST OF THE REBEL NOBLES WERE THERE.

WITHIN SIX DAYS, THE CASTLE SURRENDERED.

IN THE WINTER OF 1176–1177, RICHARD MARCHED SOUTH AND DEFEATED THE REMAINING REBELS.

WITH THE REBELLION CRUSHED, RICHARD PAID HIS MERCENARIES.

IT'S TIME FOR YOU TO GO HOME.

THE MERCENARIES SAW THAT THE COUNTRYSIDE WAS DEFENSELESS AND CONTINUED TO FIGHT.

NOBLES AND PEASANTS JOINED FORCES TO BATTLE THE MERCENARIES.

FOLLOW THE CROSS AND RID OUR LAND OF THE FOREIGN DEVILS!

THE MERCENARIES WERE SLAUGHTERED.

FOR NOW, AQUITAINE WAS AT PEACE.

BY DECEMBER 1177, KING HENRY II WAS THE STRONGEST RULER IN WESTERN EUROPE. HE AND HIS SONS CELEBRATED CHRISTMAS WITH A HUGE GATHERING OF LOYAL NOBLES.

BUT BY CHRISTMAS 1178, THERE WAS NEW TROUBLE IN AQUITAINE. RICHARD MOVED FAST AND CAPTURED FIVE REBEL CASTLES. IN MAY 1179, HE TOOK ON HIS GREATEST CHALLENGE TO DATE. HE LAID SIEGE TO TAILLEBOURG. EVERYONE SAID THAT THIS FORT COULD NOT BE TAKEN.

PART OF RICHARD'S ARMY BOMBARDED THE FORT. ANOTHER FORCE WAS SENT TO DESTROY THE SURROUNDING FARMLAND.

THEY'RE BURNING OUR CROPS!

THE REBELS DID **EXACTLY** WHAT RICHARD WANTED. THEY CHARGED OUT OF THE FORT. ITS GATES WERE LEFT UNDEFENDED. RICHARD LED THE ATTACK AND FORCED HIS WAY INSIDE.

WHEN HE RETURNED TO ENGLAND, HE WAS GIVEN A HERO'S WELCOME BY HIS FATHER.

IN SEPTEMBER 1180, LOUIS VII DIED. HIS 15-YEAR-OLD SON WAS CROWNED KING PHILIP II.

I WILL MAKE FRANCE GREAT AGAIN.

IN SPRING 1182, RICHARD HELPED HIS FATHER AND OLDER BROTHER STOP ANOTHER REBELLION IN AQUITAINE.

TOGETHER, THE ANGEVIN FAMILY SEEMED **UNBEATABLE.** BUT TROUBLE WAS BREWING AGAIN WITH HENRY THE YOUNGER.

RICHARD HAS AQUITAINE. GEOFFREY HAS BRITTANY. BUT YOU STILL COMMAND THE LANDS YOU HAVE GIVEN ME!

PATIENCE! WHEN I DIE YOU WILL BE LORD OF ALL THE LANDS!

BUT YOU'RE ONLY 49! LET ME RULE NORMANDY!

NO!

I'VE HAD ENOUGH! I'M LEAVING!

HENRY THE YOUNGER THEN PLOTTED WITH REBELS FROM AQUITAINE.

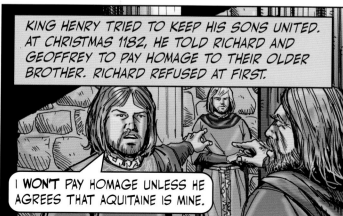

KING HENRY TRIED TO KEEP HIS SONS UNITED. AT CHRISTMAS 1182, HE TOLD RICHARD AND GEOFFREY TO PAY HOMAGE TO THEIR OLDER BROTHER. RICHARD REFUSED AT FIRST.

I **WON'T** PAY HOMAGE UNLESS HE AGREES THAT AQUITAINE IS MINE.

BUT WHEN RICHARD CHANGED HIS MIND...

I **CANNOT** ACCEPT YOUR HOMAGE. I SUPPORT THE REBELS OF AQUITAINE!

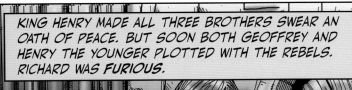

KING HENRY MADE ALL THREE BROTHERS SWEAR AN OATH OF PEACE. BUT SOON BOTH GEOFFREY AND HENRY THE YOUNGER PLOTTED WITH THE REBELS. RICHARD WAS **FURIOUS**.

NOW THEY **BOTH** WANT TO TAKE AQUITAINE AWAY FROM ME.

RICHARD WAS NOT GOING TO GIVE UP HIS LANDS WITHOUT A FIGHT. HE PREPARED HIS CASTLES AND KNIGHTS FOR BATTLE.

THINGS WENT WELL AT FIRST. IN FEBRUARY 1183, RICHARD AND A SMALL TROOP OF HIS KNIGHTS DEFEATED ONE OF THE REBELS' ARMIES.

KING HENRY RODE SOUTH TO TRY TO MAKE PEACE. BUT HE WAS NEARLY KILLED BY REBELS WHO DID NOT RECOGNIZE HIS ROYAL BANNER.

ALTHOUGH RICHARD AND HIS FATHER NOW JOINED FORCES, THEIR ENEMIES SEEMED TO HAVE THE UPPER HAND. THE FRENCH KING, PHILIP II, SENT A FORCE TO AID THE REBEL BROTHERS, HENRY THE YOUNGER AND GEOFFREY. MORE AND MORE REBEL NOBLES JOINED THEIR CAUSE.

THEN FATE TOOK A HAND. HENRY THE YOUNGER BECAME ILL IN MAY 1183. HE DIED IN JUNE. HIS CLAIM TO AQUITAINE DIED WITH HIM. THE REBELS NO LONGER HAD A REASON TO FIGHT. THE WAR WAS SOON OVER.

RICHARD WAS NOW HEIR TO THE ENGLISH THRONE. GEOFFREY WAS PUNISHED BY HAVING HIS CASTLES IN BRITTANY TAKEN AWAY. THE YOUNGEST BROTHER, JOHN, STILL HAD NO LAND OF HIS OWN.

IN SEPTEMBER 1183, KING HENRY CALLED RICHARD AND JOHN TO HIS COURT.

RICHARD WAS ORDERED TO GIVE AQUITAINE TO JOHN. IN RETURN, JOHN WAS TO PAY HIM HOMAGE.

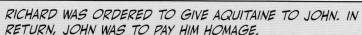

IF YOU ARE TO STEP INTO YOUR DEAD BROTHER'S SHOES AS MY HEIR, THEN JOHN SHOULD STEP INTO **YOURS.**

ALLOW ME A FEW DAYS TO THINK ABOUT IT, FATHER.

RICHARD LEFT FOR AQUITAINE. HE SENT A MESSENGER TO HIS FATHER.

TELL HIM I SHALL **NEVER** GIVE UP AQUITAINE!

KING HENRY TRIED TO GET RICHARD TO CHANGE HIS MIND. FINALLY, THE KING'S PATIENCE REACHED ITS END.

JOHN, GET AN ARMY AND TAKE AQUITAINE **BY FORCE!**

AS JOHN WAS ONLY 16, GEOFFREY LED THE ATTACK ON AQUITAINE IN JUNE 1184.

BY NOW, BRITTANY WAS GEOFFREY'S AGAIN. RICHARD TOOK HIS REVENGE ON GEOFFREY BY ATTACKING HIS CASTLES THERE.

WHEN NEWS REACHED KING HENRY OF THE BROTHERS' WAR, HE CALLED ALL THREE OF THEM TO ENGLAND. THEY WERE FORCED TO MAKE UP.

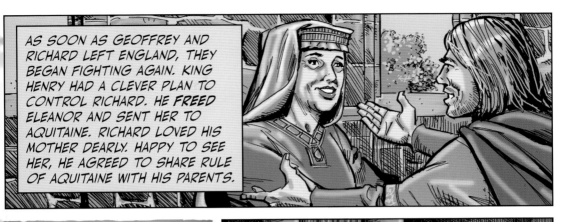

AS SOON AS GEOFFREY AND RICHARD LEFT ENGLAND, THEY BEGAN FIGHTING AGAIN. KING HENRY HAD A CLEVER PLAN TO CONTROL RICHARD. HE **FREED** ELEANOR AND SENT HER TO AQUITAINE. RICHARD LOVED HIS MOTHER DEARLY. HAPPY TO SEE HER, HE AGREED TO SHARE RULE OF AQUITAINE WITH HIS PARENTS.

IN MARCH 1186, KING HENRY AND KING PHILIP OF FRANCE AGREED THAT RICHARD SHOULD MARRY PHILIP'S SISTER, ALICE. ALICE HAD BEEN LIVING IN ENGLAND SINCE 1169, UNDER KING HENRY'S PROTECTION.* HENRY HOPED TO GAIN FRENCH LANDS IF ALICE MARRIED ONE OF HIS SONS.

*THERE WERE RUMORS THAT HENRY AND ALICE WERE IN LOVE.

THE AGREEMENT DID NOT STOP PHILIP FROM PLOTTING WITH GEOFFREY AGAINST RICHARD.

THAT GEOFFREY OF BRITTANY IS MAKING TROUBLE!

BUT IN AUGUST, AT A TOURNAMENT IN PARIS...

GEOFFREY! WATCH OUT!

AAAAARGH!

HOW IS HE?

HE'S DEAD, SIRE.

KING PHILIP NOW LAID CLAIM TO GEOFFREY'S BRITTANY. HE ALSO INSISTED THAT ALICE BE MARRIED OR RETURNED TO HIS COURT. KING HENRY DID NOT WANT TO DO EITHER.

IF WE KEEP HER HERE, PHILIP WON'T BE ABLE TO MARRY HER OFF TO ANYONE ELSE.

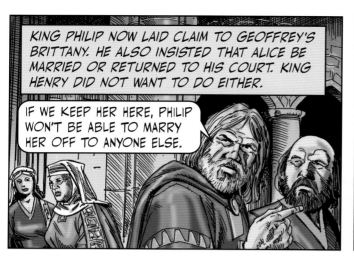

IN JUNE 1187, KING PHILIP'S ARMY INVADED BERRY IN EASTERN AQUITAINE.

RICHARD AND JOHN STOPPED THE FRENCH FORCES AT CHÂTEAUROUX.

MY LORDS, KING HENRY AND HIS ARMY ARE ONLY A DAY'S MARCH AWAY.

WHEN KING HENRY'S ARMY ARRIVED, THEY FOUND KING PHILIP'S ARMY READY FOR BATTLE.

THE TWO ARMIES MET FOR AN ALL-OUT BATTLE. BUT AT THE LAST MINUTE, BOTH BACKED DOWN.*

*AT THIS TIME IN HISTORY, IT WAS RARE FOR ARMIES TO COMMIT TO LARGE BATTLES. SIEGES WERE THE MOST COMMON WAY OF WAGING WAR.

THE TWO SIDES COULD NOT AGREE ON PEACE TERMS. INSTEAD, THEY SETTLED ON A TWO-YEAR TRUCE.*

*A TRUCE IS A TEMPORARY BREAK IN THE FIGHTING DURING A WAR.

RICHARD AND PHILIP HAD BECOME GOOD FRIENDS DURING THE TALKS. WHEN PHILIP LEFT FOR PARIS, RICHARD WENT WITH HIM.

KING HENRY WAS DEEPLY ALARMED.

HOW DARE RICHARD SIDE WITH THE ENEMY!

A FEW WEEKS LATER, NEWS ARRIVED FROM THE HOLY LAND. JERUSALEM HAD BEEN **CAPTURED** BY THE ARMY OF THE MUSLIM RULER, **SALADIN.**

IN AUTUMN 1187, RICHARD **TOOK THE CROSS** IN THE CATHEDRAL OF TOURS.*

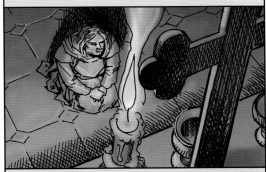

*TAKING THE CROSS WAS THE PROMISE A KNIGHT MADE TO GO ON A CRUSADE.

KING HENRY WAS STUNNED WHEN HE HEARD OF HIS SON'S ACT. PHILIP WAS NOT HAPPY EITHER. HE WANTED RICHARD TO MARRY ALICE AS SOON AS POSSIBLE. THE TWO KINGS MET IN JANUARY 1188 TO SETTLE THEIR DIFFERENCES. BUT AFTER LISTENING TO A FIERY CHURCH SERMON, HENRY AND PHILIP ALSO TOOK THE CROSS.

ORGANIZING A CRUSADE WAS EXPENSIVE. A TAX WAS STARTED TO RAISE MONEY. AFTER IT WAS ANNOUNCED THAT KNIGHTS WHO WENT ON CRUSADE DID NOT HAVE TO PAY THE TAX, MANY KNIGHTS TOOK THE CROSS!

RICHARD DID NOT GO TO THE HOLY LAND RIGHT AWAY. HE STILL HAD TROUBLES AT HOME.

BAD NEWS, MY LORD. THERE IS REBELLION IN AQUITAINE ONCE MORE.

NOT AGAIN!

IT WAS EARLY 1188. RICHARD DEALT WITH THE REBELS IN HIS USUAL FASHION – HE DESTROYED EACH CASTLE HE CAPTURED.

BEFORE LONG, THE REBELS WERE ASKING FOR PEACE. RICHARD AGREED, BUT THEIR PUNISHMENT WAS TO TAKE UP THE CROSS.

THERE WAS ALSO TROUBLE IN TOULOUSE, SOUTHEAST OF AQUITAINE.

IT'S TIME WE TAUGHT THE COUNT OF TOULOUSE A LESSON!

RICHARD ATTACKED WITH A LARGE FORCE OF MERCENARIES AND CAPTURED 17 CASTLES.

THE COUNT ASKED KING PHILIP OF FRANCE FOR HELP, AND...

...PHILIP SENT A MESSENGER TO KING HENRY...

TELL KING PHILIP THAT RICHARD IS ACTING ALONE, WITHOUT MY SUPPORT.

YOUR SON HAS NO RIGHT TO ATTACK TOULOUSE.

KING PHILIP TOOK MATTERS INTO HIS OWN HANDS. HE INVADED BERRY AGAIN AND QUICKLY CAPTURED SEVERAL CASTLES. KING HENRY WAS SO ALARMED THAT HE SAILED FROM ENGLAND TO NORMANDY. PHILIP WAS FORCED NORTH TO FACE HENRY'S ARMY THERE.

RICHARD BEGAN RECAPTURING HIS CASTLES IN BERRY. AS USUAL, HE WAS IN THE THICK OF THE FIGHTING. AT ONE POINT, HE WAS THROWN FROM HIS HORSE...

AAAARGH!

I HAVE YOU, MY LORD.

AS THE WAR DRAGGED ON, NOBLES ON BOTH SIDES GREW LESS AND LESS WILLING TO FIGHT OTHERS WHO HAD TAKEN UP THE CROSS. IN OCTOBER 1188, RICHARD AND THE TWO KINGS MET FOR PEACE TALKS. KING HENRY COULD NOT AGREE ON TERMS AND BROKE OFF THE TALKS.

RICHARD DECIDED TO TALK DIRECTLY WITH KING PHILIP. AFTER SETTLING THEIR DIFFERENCES, THEY ARRANGED TO MEET KING HENRY. WHEN HENRY SAW PHILIP AND RICHARD ARRIVING TOGETHER, HE WAS *FURIOUS*.

HE SIDES WITH MY ENEMY **AGAIN!**

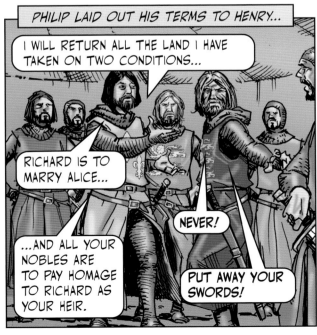

PHILIP LAID OUT HIS TERMS TO HENRY...

I WILL RETURN ALL THE LAND I HAVE TAKEN ON TWO CONDITIONS...

RICHARD IS TO MARRY ALICE...

NEVER!

...AND ALL YOUR NOBLES ARE TO PAY HOMAGE TO RICHARD AS YOUR HEIR.

PUT AWAY YOUR SWORDS!

RICHARD KNELT TO PHILIP...

THEN I PAY HOMAGE FOR ALL MY LANDS TO **PHILIP,** KING OF FRANCE.*

UNBELIEVABLE!

*HENRY AND RICHARD WERE VERY POWERFUL. IN FRANCE, HOWEVER, THEIR LORD WAS STILL PHILIP, THE RIGHTFUL KING.

RICHARD WAS DETERMINED TO HOLD ONTO HIS FRENCH LANDS, EVEN IF IT MEANT BETRAYING HIS FATHER. THE THREE MEN AGREED ON ANOTHER TRUCE AND TO MEET AGAIN IN JANUARY 1189. REFUSING TO MAKE UP WITH HENRY, RICHARD LEFT FOR AQUITAINE.

KING HENRY SPENT CHRISTMAS 1188 IN ANJOU AT HIS CASTLE OF SAUMUR.

YOU DO NOT LOOK WELL, MY LORD.

I AM **WORN OUT.**

HENRY BECAME ILL AND MISSED THE JANUARY MEETING.

PHILIP AND RICHARD THOUGHT KING HENRY WAS LYING – BOTH ABOUT HIS ILLNESS AND ABOUT HIS FUTURE PLANS.

HE WON'T LET JOHN TAKE THE CROSS. PERHAPS HE PLANS TO MAKE **JOHN** HIS HEIR INSTEAD OF **YOU.**

HENRY SENT MANY MESSENGERS TO RICHARD. HE HOPED TO CALL HIM BACK TO HIS SIDE...

YOUR FATHER IS SORRY HE OFFENDED YOU.

I NO LONGER BELIEVE ANYTHING HE SAYS. HE HAS LOST MY TRUST.

IN EARLY SUMMER, THE POPE SENT A PEACEMAKING MISSION TO FRANCE, AND...

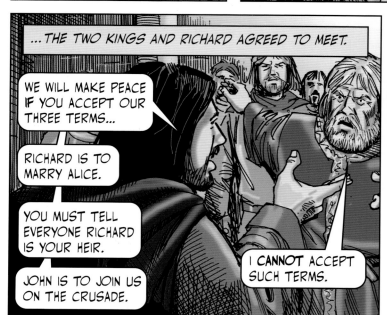

...THE TWO KINGS AND RICHARD AGREED TO MEET.

WE WILL MAKE PEACE IF YOU ACCEPT OUR THREE TERMS...

RICHARD IS TO MARRY ALICE.

YOU MUST TELL EVERYONE RICHARD IS YOUR HEIR.

JOHN IS TO JOIN US ON THE CRUSADE.

I **CANNOT** ACCEPT SUCH TERMS.

THEN WE ARE AT WAR.

RICHARD AND PHILIP INVADED MAINE AND QUICKLY CAPTURED FIVE OF HENRY'S CASTLES. THEN THEY HEADED FOR LE MANS, THE TOWN HENRY WAS STAYING IN – AND THE PLACE WHERE HE HAD BEEN BORN.

HENRY'S FAITHFUL KNIGHT, WILLIAM MARSHAL, ARRANGED HENRY'S RETREAT AND TOOK COMMAND OF THE KING'S REAR GUARD.

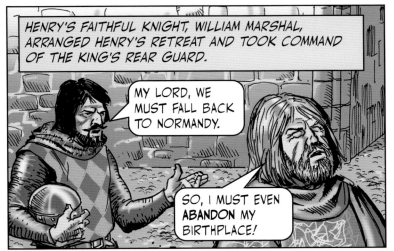

MY LORD, WE MUST FALL BACK TO NORMANDY.

SO, I MUST EVEN **ABANDON** MY BIRTHPLACE!

GO WITH THE KING. I WILL PROTECT HIS BACK.

RICHARD CHASED HENRY AND CAUGHT UP WITH THE REAR GUARD.

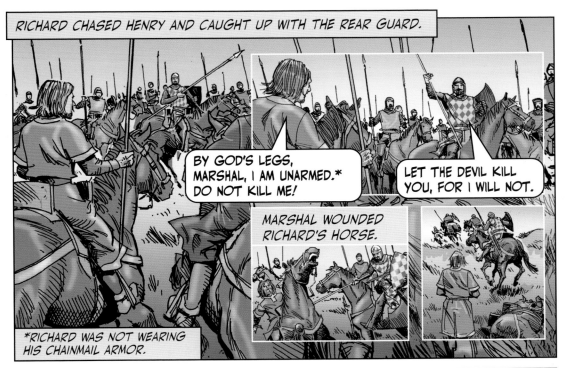

BY GOD'S LEGS, MARSHAL, I AM UNARMED.* DO NOT KILL ME!

LET THE DEVIL KILL YOU, FOR I WILL NOT.

MARSHAL WOUNDED RICHARD'S HORSE.

*RICHARD WAS NOT WEARING HIS CHAINMAIL ARMOR.

HENRY ESCAPED BUT WAS TOO ILL TO REACH NORMANDY. INSTEAD, HE TURNED SOUTH FOR CHINON CASTLE IN TOURAINE. BY JULY, RICHARD AND PHILIP CONTROLLED MAINE AND TOURAINE. HENRY WAS FORCED TO AGREE TO THEIR PEACE TERMS.

GOD GRANT THAT I MAY NOT DIE UNTIL I HAVE HAD MY **REVENGE** ON YOU.

KING HENRY DIED AT CHINON ON JULY 6, 1189. HIS FINAL HOURS WERE MADE EVEN WORSE BY THE NEWS THAT JOHN HAD JOINED RICHARD IN REBELLING AGAINST HIM.

HENRY'S BODY WAS TAKEN TO THE ABBEY CHURCH AT NEARBY FONTEVRAUD. RICHARD, THE NEW KING OF ENGLAND, WENT TO PAY HIS RESPECTS.

SO, MARSHAL, THE OTHER DAY YOU TRIED TO KILL ME.

IF I HAD WANTED TO, I WOULD HAVE.

MARSHAL, YOU ARE PARDONED. I BEAR YOU NO BAD FEELING.

FROM THAT DAY, WILLIAM MARSHAL WOULD BE RICHARD'S MOST LOYAL KNIGHT.

RICHARD INHERITED ALL THE ANGEVINS' FRENCH LANDS. INSTEAD OF PUNISHING THE DEAD KING'S FOLLOWERS, THE NEW KING KEPT HIS FATHER'S PROMISES TO THEM. AT A MEETING WITH PHILIP, RICHARD AGAIN PROMISED TO MARRY ALICE – BUT DID NOT SET A DATE. PHILIP GAVE BACK MOST OF THE LANDS HE HAD CAPTURED.

RICHARD THEN SAILED FOR ENGLAND. HE LANDED AT PORTSMOUTH IN AUGUST 1189. HE WAS GIVEN A WARM WELCOME.

IN LONDON, HE WAS CROWNED KING RICHARD I OF ENGLAND ON SEPTEMBER 13.

RICHARD SPENT THE REST OF 1189 ESTABLISHING HIS RULE IN ENGLAND AND RAISING MONEY TO PAY FOR HIS CRUSADE. HE GAVE HIS BROTHER JOHN, WHO WAS NOT GOING WITH HIM TO THE HOLY LAND, VAST AREAS OF ENGLISH LAND ALONG WITH THEIR CASTLES, INCLUDING NOTTINGHAM. RICHARD MADE SURE HIS BROTHER WAS RICH IN LAND, BUT NOT POWER.

IN DECEMBER 1189, RICHARD SAILED FOR FRANCE.

MAY GOD GO WITH YOU.

ON DECEMBER 30, RICHARD AND PHILIP MET...

WHEN ARE YOU GOING TO SET A DATE FOR THE MARRIAGE?

ALICE IS A WONDERFUL WOMAN. BUT I HAVE SO MANY OTHER THINGS TO TEND TO.

RICHARD AND ELEANOR WERE **SECRETLY** WORKING ON ANOTHER MARRIAGE PLAN. THIS PLAN WOULD HELP SOLVE A PROBLEM – THE COUNT OF TOULOUSE WAS NOT GOING ON CRUSADE.

HE'S **BOUND** TO ATTACK AQUITAINE AGAIN WHILE I'M AWAY.

WE NEED A POWERFUL ALLY TO FIGHT ON OUR SIDE.

KING ALFONSO OF ARAGON IS THE COUNT'S ENEMY.*

AND KING SANCHO OF NAVARRE IS ALFONSO'S FRIEND. MARRYING SANCHO'S ELDEST DAUGHTER, BERENGARIA, WOULD GAIN YOU TWO ALLIES.*

PLEASE ARRANGE IT, MOTHER.

*ARAGON AND NAVARRE WERE SPANISH KINGDOMS.

IN JUNE 1190, RICHARD RECEIVED THE PILGRIM'S STAFF IN THE CATHEDRAL OF TOURS.

OOPS!

SNAP

HE THEN TRAVELED EAST TO VÉZELAY, WHERE HE MET WITH KING PHILIP.

SINCE WE WILL CONQUER NEW LANDS AS WELL AS FREE JERUSALEM, LET US AGREE TO SPLIT OUR GAINS EQUALLY.

THE TWO KINGS AND THEIR ARMIES SET OFF ON JULY 4. THEIR CRUSADE HAD BEGUN.

PHILIP WAS TO SAIL FROM GENOA, ITALY. RICHARD HEADED FOR THE FRENCH PORT OF MARSEILLE, WHERE HE WAS EXPECTING TO FIND SHIPS WAITING FOR HIS ARMY. WHEN HE ARRIVED, THERE WAS NO SIGN OF THE SHIPS. RICHARD HIRED SHIPS AND DIVIDED HIS ARMY IN TWO. ONE HALF SAILED DIRECTLY FOR THE HOLY LAND. IT REACHED TYRE ON SEPTEMBER 16, 1190.

RICHARD SAILED FOR ITALY WITH THE REST OF HIS ARMY. HIS FIRST STOP WAS GENOA, WHERE HE VISITED PHILIP. THE KINGS ARGUED. THE QUARREL BEGAN WHEN PHILIP ASKED A FAVOR...

CAN YOU LEND ME SHIPS? I NEED FIVE.

I CAN ONLY LET YOU HAVE THREE.

BAH! IN THAT CASE, I WON'T TAKE ANY!

BY LATE SEPTEMBER, RICHARD WAS IN ITALY'S FAR SOUTH. HE HAD A NARROW ESCAPE ONE DAY, WHEN EXPLORING WITH A COMPANION...

SCREECH

THAT SOUNDS LIKE A HAWK!*

*ONLY NOBLES WERE ALLOWED TO OWN HAWKS AT THIS TIME.

IT IS A HAWK, AND A FINE ONE AT THAT.

HUH!

IT LOOKS LIKE THEY WANT THE BIRD BACK.

I WILL NOT RETURN A HAWK TO A BUNCH OF PEASANTS!

SK-AANG

QUICK, MY LORD! MOUNT YOUR HORSE.

HAHAHA

THE NEXT DAY, RICHARD REACHED MESSINA, SICILY. PHILIP HAD BEEN THERE FOR A WEEK.

LOOK AT RICHARD. HE IS SO POMPOUS!

RICHARD AND HIS ARMY SET UP CAMP.

THEN HE DEALT WITH TANCRED, THE NEW KING OF SICILY.

RICHARD'S SISTER JOAN HAD BEEN MARRIED TO THE OLD KING WHO DIED. TANCRED WAS HOLDING JOAN PRISONER. HE ALSO OWED HER MONEY, SHIPS, AND OTHER GOODS. RICHARD MADE TANCRED SET JOAN FREE AND RETURN THE MONEY AND SHIPS. HE THEN CAPTURED BAGNARA ON THE MAINLAND FOR JOAN TO LIVE IN.

THE SICILIANS WERE WORRIED THAT THE CRUSADERS WOULD TAKE OVER THEIR ISLAND. THE CRUSADERS ALSO CAUSED FOOD SHORTAGES. THE BAD FEELINGS LED TO FULL BATTLE.

LEADING HIS MEN, RICHARD **STORMED** THE GATES OF MESSINA.

PHILIP'S MEN STOOD BY AND WATCHED AS RICHARD CAPTURED THE CITY.

BUT PHILIP WAS FURIOUS WHEN HE SAW RICHARD'S BANNERS FLYING OVER THE CITY.

I **DEMAND** YOU TAKE THEM DOWN AND RAISE MY BANNERS INSTEAD!

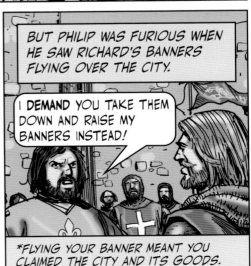

*FLYING YOUR BANNER MEANT YOU CLAIMED THE CITY AND ITS GOODS.

RICHARD REFUSED, AND PHILIP GREW ANGRIER. TANCRED HAD TO HAND OVER MORE MONEY AFTER RICHARD TOOK MESSINA. HE USED IT TO FUND HIS CRUSADE AND BUY PEACE WITH PHILIP – THE FRENCH KING WAS GIVEN A THIRD OF THE MONEY.

RICHARD GAVE BACK MESSINA TO TANCRED AND PROMISED TO BE HIS ALLY. EVERYONE SEEMED HAPPY BY THE TIME RICHARD HELD A HUGE FEAST TO CELEBRATE CHRISTMAS 1190.

BUT RICHARD'S ARMY IN THE HOLY LAND WAS **STARVING**...

MEANWHILE, BERENGARIA WAS ON HER WAY TO SICILY TO MARRY RICHARD – AND PHILIP KNEW IT. FURIOUS, HE TOLD TANCRED THAT RICHARD WAS NOT A MAN OF HIS WORD. RICHARD ARGUED WITH PHILIP...

WHY ARE YOU SPREADING **LIES** ABOUT ME!

YOU HAVE **BROKEN** YOUR WORD ABOUT MARRYING ALICE!

I **CAN'T** MARRY HER. SHE WAS MY FATHER'S COMPANION.

TO FREE HIMSELF FROM MARRYING ALICE, RICHARD GAVE PHILIP MORE MONEY. PHILIP ACCEPTED IT, BUT HIS FEELINGS TOWARD RICHARD DEVELOPED INTO HATRED.

PHILIP SET SAIL FOR THE HOLY LAND IN MARCH 1191. WITHIN HOURS, BERENGARIA REACHED SICILY. SHE WAS WITH RICHARD'S MOTHER, ELEANOR.

ELEANOR RETURNED TO AQUITAINE A FEW DAYS LATER. RICHARD HAD ALREADY GOTTEN HIS ARMY READY TO LEAVE SICILY. DECIDING TO HOLD THE WEDDING IN CYPRUS, HE SET SAIL ON APRIL 10.

CYPRUS WAS A KEY SUPPLY BASE FOR EUROPEANS SAILING TO THE HOLY LAND. IT WAS RULED BY ISAAC COMNENUS, WHO FEARED THAT RICHARD PLANNED TO CAPTURE IT. ISAAC ASKED FOR HELP FROM THE MUSLIM RULER, SALADIN.

A FEW DAYS OUT AT SEA, RICHARD'S SHIPS WERE SPLIT UP BY A STORM. SOME SHIPS REACHED CYPRUS SAFELY ON APRIL 24. THREE WERE WRECKED OFF LIMASSOL. THEIR CARGOES WERE STOLEN AND THE SURVIVORS WERE PUT IN PRISON.

RICHARD AND SOME OF HIS SHIPS REACHED LIMASSOL ON MAY 6. ISAAC'S ARMY WERE WAITING FOR THEM.

RICHARD AND HIS MEN PILED INTO BOATS AND ROWED FOR THE SHORE.

RICHARD'S MEN LET FLY WITH THEIR ARROWS FROM THE BOATS...

AS SOON AS HE SET FOOT ON DRY LAND, RICHARD **LED THE CHARGE** UP THE BEACH.

AFTER FIERCE FIGHTING, ISAAC'S ARMY RETREATED.

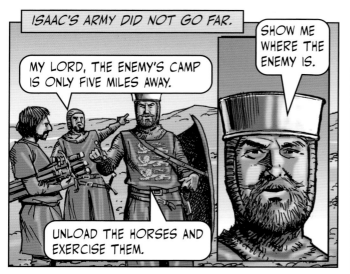

ISAAC'S ARMY DID NOT GO FAR.

MY LORD, THE ENEMY'S CAMP IS ONLY FIVE MILES AWAY.

SHOW ME WHERE THE ENEMY IS.

UNLOAD THE HORSES AND EXERCISE THEM.

WE'LL ATTACK THEM WHILE THEY SLEEP.

THERE ARE ONLY 50 HORSES READY, MY LORD.

THAT WILL BE ENOUGH.

BUT, SIRE, THERE ARE HUNDREDS OF THE ENEMY.

YOU GET ON WITH YOUR WORK. **LEAVE THE FIGHTING TO US!**

RICHARD'S ATTACK WAS SO FIERCE AND UNEXPECTED THAT ISAAC BARELY ESCAPED WITH HIS LIFE.

AFTER RICHARD'S TWO VICTORIES IN 24 HOURS, MOST ENEMY NOBLES IN CYPRUS WERE **EAGER** TO PAY HOMAGE TO HIM. ISAAC WAS ALSO READY TO MAKE PEACE.

RICHARD MARRIED BERENGARIA THE NEXT DAY.

ISAAC AGREED TO RICHARD'S PEACE TERMS AND PAID HOMAGE TO HIM.

THE TERMS WERE STIFF, MY LORD.

YES, AND I DOUBT THAT ISAAC WILL KEEP THEM.

BY NOW, PHILIP WAS IN THE HOLY LAND, STIRRING UP TROUBLE. BACK IN 1187, SALADIN HAD OVERTHROWN THE CHRISTIAN KING OF JERUSALEM, GUY OF LUSIGNAN. GUY WAS RELATED TO RICHARD BY MARRIAGE...

GREETINGS, GUY. WHAT NEWS FROM THE HOLY LAND?

I NEED YOUR HELP, SIRE. PHILIP PLANS TO MAKE CONRAD OF MONTFERRAT KING OF JERUSALEM IN MY PLACE.

RICHARD AGREED, IN RETURN FOR HELP WITH THE CONQUEST OF CYPRUS. GUY WAS TO TAKE PART OF RICHARD'S ARMY AND GO OVERLAND AFTER ISAAC. RICHARD AND HIS MEN WERE TO SAIL AROUND THE ISLAND, CAPTURING SHIPS, COASTAL TOWNS, AND CASTLES.

ISAAC AND HIS FOLLOWERS FELL BACK TO HIS CASTLES IN THE MOUNTAINS. BUT THEN GUY CAPTURED ISAAC'S DAUGHTER. THE NEWS BROKE ISAAC'S HEART. ON JUNE 1, HE SET THE TERMS FOR HIS SURRENDER.

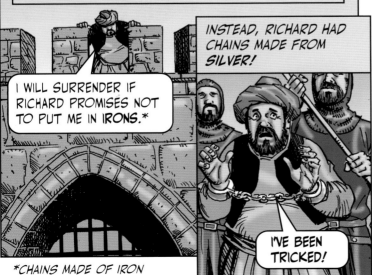

I WILL SURRENDER IF RICHARD PROMISES NOT TO PUT ME IN IRONS.*

INSTEAD, RICHARD HAD CHAINS MADE FROM SILVER!

I'VE BEEN TRICKED!

*CHAINS MADE OF IRON

RICHARD SOLD CYPRUS TO THE TEMPLARS.* THE ISLAND WOULD BE IN FRIENDLY HANDS. THE MONEY WOULD HELP PAY FOR THE CRUSADE. ON JUNE 5, 1190, RICHARD AND HIS ARMY SET SAIL FOR TYRE IN THE HOLY LAND.

*THE TEMPLARS WERE A RICH AND POWERFUL ORDER OF CHRISTIAN KNIGHTS.

31

TYRE WAS STILL IN CHRISTIAN HANDS. ACRE, A FEW MILES TO ITS SOUTH, WAS HELD BY SALADIN. AS THE REGION'S LARGEST PORT, ACRE WAS IMPORTANT TO BOTH SIDES. THE CRUSADERS HAD BEEN TRYING TO CAPTURE IT SINCE 1189. BUT THEIR ARMY WAS NOT LARGE ENOUGH TO BREAK ITS DEFENSES.

AFTER REACHING TYRE ON JUNE 7, RICHARD SAILED TO ACRE WITH PART OF HIS ARMY.

ONE OF SALADIN'S TOP COMMANDERS WAS IN CHARGE OF ACRE'S DEFENSE.

TAKE WORD OF THE NEWCOMERS TO SALADIN.

YES, MY LORD. RIGHT AWAY.

SALADIN WAS CAMPED A FEW MILES OUTSIDE ACRE.

THE CRUSADERS WERE USING GIANT **CATAPULTS** TO TOSS ROCKS AND OTHER OBJECTS AT THE CITY'S WALLS.

PHILIP WANTED RICHARD'S ARMY TO JOIN HIM IN A LARGE ATTACK ON ACRE.

RICHARD REFUSED. INSTEAD, HE ORDERED HIS MEN TO BRING THEIR CATAPULTS AND JOIN THE BOMBARDMENT.

THE WALLS OF ACRE WERE SLOWLY BEING **BATTERED** DOWN. THE CITY'S MUSLIM DEFENDERS WERE EXHAUSTED.

THEY GOT RELIEF WHEN RICHARD AND THEN PHILIP BECAME ILL.

MEANWHILE, RICHARD HAD BEEN TRYING TO ARRANGE A MEETING WITH SALADIN. SALADIN REFUSED, BUT SENT HIS BROTHER, AL-ADIL...

WE MUST GET INSIDE THEIR MINDS AND LEARN HOW THEY THINK.

RICHARD HAD HIS BED CARRIED TO THE FRONT LINE. HERE, HE DIRECTED THE ATTACK AND SHOWED OFF HIS SKILL WITH A CROSSBOW.

EXCELLENT SHOT, MY LORD.

THE CRUSADERS KEPT UP THEIR BOMBARDMENT, NIGHT AND DAY. THE MUSLIMS FOUGHT ON WITH GREAT COURAGE UNTIL ACRE **SURRENDERED** ON JULY 12.

RICHARD AND PHILIP AGREED TO DIVIDE THE CITY AND ITS CONTENTS BETWEEN THEM. THEIR MEN TOOK MORE THAN 3,000 MUSLIM PRISONERS.

MANY KNIGHTS DEMANDED A SHARE OF THE CITY'S WEALTH. BOTH KINGS REFUSED THEM. MANY OF THESE KNIGHTS SOLD THEIR WEAPONS AND LEFT THE CRUSADE.

PHILIP HAD HAD ENOUGH OF BOTH RICHARD AND THE HOLY LAND. ON AUGUST 3, THE FRENCH KING SET SAIL FROM TYRE. HE LEFT MOST OF HIS ARMY TO SUPPORT THE CRUSADE.

BEFORE PHILIP LEFT, HE AND RICHARD SETTLED THE QUESTION OF JERUSALEM'S KING. GUY OF LUSIGNAN WAS TO HOLD THE TITLE UNTIL HIS DEATH. THEN IT WAS TO PASS TO CONRAD OF MONTFERRAT. WITH PHILIP GONE, RICHARD WAS NOW THE CRUSADE'S ONLY LEADER. HIS FIRST TASK WAS TO MAKE SURE SALADIN MET THE AGREED PEACE TERMS. ON AUGUST 11, THE MUSLIM LEADER WAS DUE TO PAY A LARGE SUM OF MONEY AND RETURN HUNDREDS OF CAPTIVE CRUSADERS. IN RETURN, RICHARD WAS TO SET FREE THE MUSLIMS CAPTURED AT ACRE.

AUGUST 11 ARRIVED, BUT NO MONEY CAME FROM SALADIN. HE MAY HAVE BEEN TRYING TO DELAY THE CRUSADERS FROM MOVING ON TO JERUSALEM. ON AUGUST 20, RICHARD ORDERED THE **DEATH** OF OVER 2,500 MUSLIM CAPTIVES.

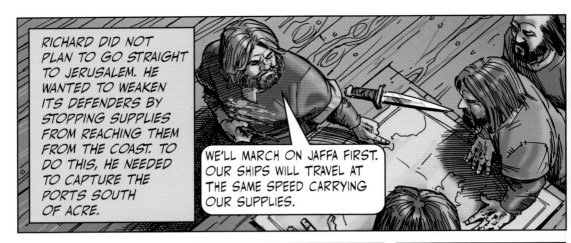

RICHARD DID NOT PLAN TO GO STRAIGHT TO JERUSALEM. HE WANTED TO WEAKEN ITS DEFENDERS BY STOPPING SUPPLIES FROM REACHING THEM FROM THE COAST. TO DO THIS, HE NEEDED TO CAPTURE THE PORTS SOUTH OF ACRE.

WE'LL MARCH ON JAFFA FIRST. OUR SHIPS WILL TRAVEL AT THE SAME SPEED CARRYING OUR SUPPLIES.

ON AUGUST 22, THE ARMY OF 14,000 CRUSADERS MARCHED.

THE WEATHER WAS BOILING HOT. THE MEN COOKED INSIDE THEIR CHAINMAIL ARMOR.

SMALL GROUPS OF SALADIN'S ARCHERS MADE HIT-AND-RUN ATTACKS...

...BUT THE CRUSADERS KEPT MARCHING SOUTHWARD. THEIR ARMOR HELPED PROTECT THEM.

THEY STILL MARCH WITH SO MANY ARROWS IN THEM.

AT ONE POINT, RICHARD WAS INJURED BY AN ENEMY ARROW...

MY LORD, YOU SHOULD NOT PUT YOURSELF IN SUCH DANGER.

I'LL BE FINE.

AS THE ARMY NEARED JAFFA, RICHARD REALIZED THAT SALADIN WOULD ATTACK WITH HIS WHOLE ARMY. HE ISSUED ORDERS THAT THE KNIGHTS SHOULD NOT CHARGE UNTIL THEY HEARD HIS SIGNAL – SIX LOUD TRUMPET BLASTS.

SALADIN ISSUED HIS BATTLE ORDERS...

PESTER THE KNIGHTS INTO ATTACKING US. ONCE THEY HAVE CHARGED TOO FAR, WE CAN PICK THEM OFF.

THE MUSLIM WARRIORS CHARGED AGAIN AND AGAIN. THE SKY WAS DARK WITH ARROWS AND SPEARS.

LET US ATTACK, MY LORD.

NO. WAIT FOR THE SIGNAL!

EVENTUALLY, TWO KNIGHTS BECAME RESTLESS AND CHARGED. THE REST QUICKLY FOLLOWED.

RICHARD SOUNDED HIS TRUMPETS. HE MANAGED TO KEEP SOME OF HIS KNIGHTS BACK IN RESERVE.

WHEN SALADIN'S MEN ATTACKED THE EXHAUSTED KNIGHTS, RICHARD LED HIS KNIGHTS FORWARD. THE ENEMY FLED.

WHILE THE CRUSADERS RESTED AT JAFFA, SALADIN TOOK HIS MAIN ARMY SOUTH TO DESTROY THE PORT OF ASCALON. RICHARD WANTED TO GO AFTER HIM, BUT MOST OF HIS KNIGHTS WANTED TO GO INLAND FOR JERUSALEM. RICHARD GAVE IN TO THEM, BUT HE WAS NOT HAPPY.

RICHARD CONTINUED CONTACT WITH SALADIN THROUGH HIS BROTHER, AL-ADIL.

I CAN ASSURE YOU, SALADIN WISHES ONLY FOR PEACE.

HE'S DELAYING SO HE CAN DESTROY MORE FORTS.

RICHARD ATTACKED SALADIN'S FORAGING PARTIES AND OFTEN LED AMBUSHES HIMSELF.* ON ONE OCCASION, RICHARD LED A SMALL GROUP OF KNIGHTS TO RESCUE A GROUP OF CRUSADERS.

MY LORD, WATCH OUT!

AAARGH!

RETREAT!

*FORAGING PARTIES WERE MEN SENT TO COLLECT FOOD AND FIREWOOD.

IF YOU MUST FIGHT, TAKE MORE KNIGHTS WITH YOU, MY LORD.

BUT RICHARD CONTINUED TO LEAD HIS KNIGHTS IN BATTLES. OFTEN HE WOULD RETURN WITH THE HEADS OF HIS ENEMY.

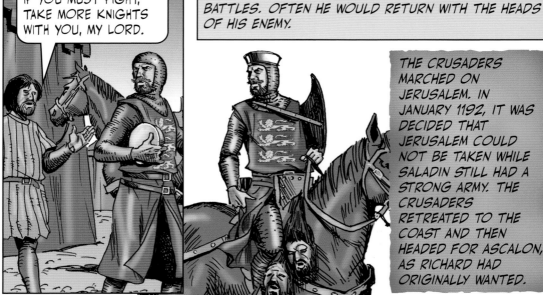

THE CRUSADERS MARCHED ON JERUSALEM. IN JANUARY 1192, IT WAS DECIDED THAT JERUSALEM COULD NOT BE TAKEN WHILE SALADIN STILL HAD A STRONG ARMY. THE CRUSADERS RETREATED TO THE COAST AND THEN HEADED FOR ASCALON, AS RICHARD HAD ORIGINALLY WANTED.

MEANWHILE, FIGHTING HAD BROKEN OUT AT ACRE BETWEEN THE ARMIES OF CONRAD AND GUY. RICHARD'S SOLUTION WAS TO MAKE CONRAD KING OF JERUSALEM. GUY WAS REPAID FOR HIS LOSS BY BEING ALLOWED TO BUY CYPRUS FROM THE TEMPLARS.

THEN, IN APRIL 1192, CONRAD WAS STABBED TO DEATH BY **ASSASSINS!***

*ASSASSINS ARE PROFESSIONAL KILLERS.

RUMORS SPREAD THAT RICHARD WAS RESPONSIBLE. BACK IN EUROPE, PHILIP GRABBED THE CHANCE TO SPREAD LIES ABOUT HIM.

RICHARD WILL BE SENDING ASSASSINS AFTER **ME** NEXT!

ASCALON WAS NOW IN THE CRUSADERS' HANDS. IN MAY 1192, RICHARD MOVED ON DARUM. HE WALKED AROUND THE DEFENSES IN FULL VIEW OF THE ARCHERS.

WITHIN A FEW DAYS, DARUM WAS CAPTURED. AT THIS POINT, RICHARD RECEIVED BAD NEWS FROM HOME.

PHILIP AND YOUR BROTHER JOHN ARE PLOTTING AGAINST YOU.

IF I CAPTURE JERUSALEM, THEY WILL NOT DARE TO MOVE AGAINST ME.

BY JUNE 10, RICHARD'S MAIN ARMY WAS CAMPED A FEW MILES FROM JERUSALEM. ONCE AGAIN, THE ATTACK WAS CALLED OFF.

SALADIN'S FORCES ARE GAINING IN STRENGTH. WE WILL BE CUT OFF FROM OUR BASE IF WE STAY HERE.

IN JUNE, RICHARD LEARNED THAT A LARGE FORCE WAS ON ITS WAY OVERLAND FROM EGYPT TO HELP SALADIN'S ARMY. RICHARD WENT AHEAD TO SPY ON THEIR CAMP...

WE'LL ATTACK IN THE MORNING.

RICHARD ATTACKED WITH JUST 1,500 MEN. THEY **CRUSHED** THE EGYPTIANS.

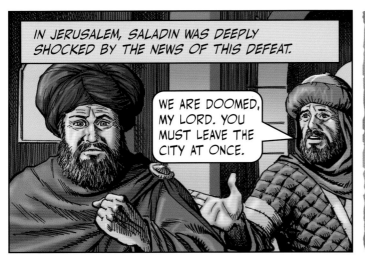

IN JERUSALEM, SALADIN WAS DEEPLY SHOCKED BY THE NEWS OF THIS DEFEAT.

WE ARE DOOMED, MY LORD. YOU MUST LEAVE THE CITY AT ONCE.

RICHARD DID NOT LAY SIEGE TO THE HOLY CITY. INSTEAD, HIS ARMY HEADED BACK TO THE COAST. WITH SALADIN'S MAIN ARMY STILL CLOSE, RICHARD THOUGHT THAT PEACE TALKS COULD STOP THE FIGHTING. SALADIN SAID HE WOULD AGREE TO RICHARD'S TERMS IF THE CRUSADERS DESTROYED ASCALON. RICHARD REFUSED.

IN LATE JULY, SALADIN MADE A SURPRISE ATTACK ON JAFFA.

RICHARD WAS IN ACRE WHEN HE HEARD THE NEWS. HE IMMEDIATELY SENT FORCES OVERLAND TO JAFFA. HE SET SAIL FOR JAFFA WITH A SECOND FORCE.

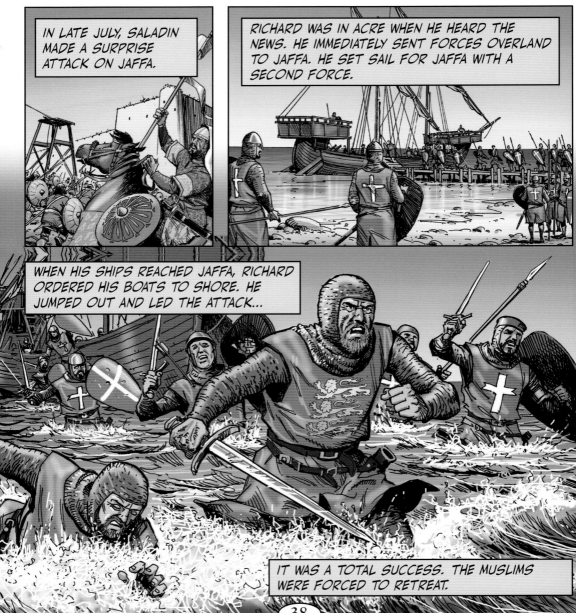

WHEN HIS SHIPS REACHED JAFFA, RICHARD ORDERED HIS BOATS TO SHORE. HE JUMPED OUT AND LED THE ATTACK...

IT WAS A TOTAL SUCCESS. THE MUSLIMS WERE FORCED TO RETREAT.

RICHARD AND HIS MEN CAMPED OUTSIDE THE CITY'S WALLS. THE OVERLAND FORCE HAD BEEN DELAYED — SALADIN SAW A CHANCE TO WIPE OUT RICHARD'S TINY FORCE. ON THE MORNING OF AUGUST 5, SALADIN LAUNCHED A SURPRISE ATTACK.

STAND STEADY, MEN.

RICHARD'S MEN HELD OFF THE ATTACK AND CLAIMED A COMPLETE VICTORY.

THE CRUSADERS STILL HELD JAFFA. BUT BY LATE AUGUST, RICHARD WAS VERY ILL.

ASK MY FRIEND SALADIN TO SEND ME FRUIT AND SNOW FROM THE MOUNTAINS.

SALADIN SENT THE GIFTS. THE TWO LEADERS BEGAN PEACE TALKS AGAIN.

REBUILDING ASCALON COST ME A FORTUNE. TELL SALADIN I WILL ONLY GIVE IT UP IF HE REPAYS MY EXPENSES.

BOTH SIDES HAD EXHAUSTED THEIR MEN AND FUNDS ON THE MANY MONTHS OF WAR. RICHARD AGREED TO GIVE UP ASCALON. IN RETURN, THE REST OF THE COASTAL REGION WAS TO BE LEFT IN THE CRUSADERS' HANDS. CHRISTIANS AND MUSLIMS WERE TO BE ALLOWED TO PASS THROUGH EACH OTHER'S LANDS. CHRISTIAN PILGRIMS WERE TO BE ALLOWED TO VISIT JERUSALEM.

ON SEPTEMBER 1, 1192, SALADIN'S BROTHER VISITED RICHARD'S BEDSIDE TO FINALIZE THE PEACE DOCUMENT. RICHARD WAS TOO ILL TO READ IT, BUT SHOOK HANDS IN AGREEMENT.

BY OCTOBER 9, RICHARD WAS WELL ENOUGH TO SET SAIL FOR HOME.

BACK IN EUROPE, PHILIP HAD BEEN CARRYING OUT A WAR OF WORDS AGAINST RICHARD. THE FRENCH KING HAD A NEW ALLY – EMPEROR HENRY VI, WHOSE LANDS STRETCHED FROM GERMANY TO ITALY.

RICHARD REALIZED HE MIGHT HAVE TROUBLE ON THE WAY HOME. HE HOPED TO KEEP HIS JOURNEY A SECRET. HE TOOK ONLY A FEW LOYAL KNIGHTS WITH HIM.

IN NOVEMBER, HIS SHIP WAS OFF THE NORTHEAST COAST OF ITALY WHEN IT WAS WRECKED BY A STORM.

RICHARD AND A FEW COMPANIONS MADE IT TO SHORE.

THESE LANDS BELONG TO EMPEROR HENRY.

YES, WE SHOULD DISGUISE OUR CLOTHES AND HOPE NO ONE NOTICES US.

A FEW DAYS LATER...

MY LORD, THERE'S A PARTY OF TRAVELERS CLAIMING TO BE PILGRIMS.

WHAT OF IT?

THEY SPEND MORE LIKE A KING!

WE'VE BEEN DISCOVERED!

WE'LL KEEP THEM BUSY WHILE YOU ESCAPE, SIRE.

HAR!

40

A FEW DAYS BEFORE CHRISTMAS 1192, RICHARD WAS CAPTURED BY EMPEROR HENRY'S COUSIN, DUKE LEOPOLD OF AUSTRIA.

TAKE HIM TO DÜRNSTEIN CASTLE!

LEOPOLD AND HENRY SPENT THE NEXT FEW MONTHS ARGUING OVER HOW TO DIVIDE UP RICHARD'S RANSOM.

SEND A MESSAGE TO PHILIP. TELL HIM OF THE JOYOUS NEWS.

ON MARCH 22, 1193, RICHARD WAS BROUGHT BEFORE HENRY AND HIS NOBLES...

YOU STAND ACCUSED OF **BETRAYING** THE HOLY LAND BY AGREEING TO PEACE TERMS WITH **SALADIN**. YOU ALSO PLOTTED TO HAVE CONRAD OF MONTFERRAT **MURDERED**.

MY LORD EMPEROR, THESE ARE LIES SPREAD BY MY ENEMY, PHILIP OF FRANCE...

RICHARD'S WORDS WON THE ENTIRE COURT OVER TO HIS SIDE.

MY NOBLES BELIEVE HIM.

RICHARD, MY FRIEND, LET US SHARE THE KISS OF PEACE.

EMPEROR HENRY SAID HE WOULD TRY TO SETTLE RICHARD AND PHILIP'S QUARREL...

...BUT RICHARD WAS FORCED TO PAY A SMALL FORTUNE FOR HIS FREEDOM.

IT IS NOT A RANSOM, KING RICHARD. IT IS, LET US SAY, MY FEE FOR ARRANGING PEACE WITH PHILIP.

HENRY TOOK NO CHANCES. HE SENT RICHARD TO TRIFELS CASTLE AND KEPT HIM UNDER CLOSE GUARD.

AFTER A WHILE, RICHARD WAS ALLOWED TO RETURN TO THE EMPEROR'S COURT. HERE, RICHARD STAYED WHILE THE RANSOM WAS RAISED. IT TOOK SOME TIME. RICHARD FINALLY RETURNED TO ENGLAND IN MARCH 1194 – 17 MONTHS AFTER HE LEFT THE HOLY LAND.

DURING RICHARD'S LONG MONTHS AS A CAPTIVE, HIS BROTHER JOHN HAD PLOTTED WITH PHILIP AND ALLOWED THE FRENCH KING TO INVADE NORMANDY. JOHN HAD ALSO TRIED TO STIR UP A REBELLION IN ENGLAND. BY THE TIME RICHARD ARRIVED HOME, JOHN HAD ESCAPED TO FRANCE AND MOST OF HIS ENGLISH CASTLES HAD SURRENDERED TO RICHARD.

ONLY NOTTINGHAM CASTLE HAD STAYED LOYAL TO JOHN. RICHARD REACHED IT IN LATE MARCH. AFTER MEN STANDING NEAR HIM WERE HIT BY ARROWS, RICHARD ORDERED AN ATTACK.

THE CASTLE SURRENDERED TWO DAYS LATER.

RICHARD SET ABOUT RE-ESTABLISHING HIS RULE IN ENGLAND. ON APRIL 17, 1194, A GREAT CEREMONY WAS HELD AT WINCHESTER. RICHARD WALKED THROUGH THE CITY WEARING HIS CROWN TO SHOW EVERYONE THAT HE WAS BACK IN ENGLAND AND IN CONTROL.

ON MAY 12, RICHARD SET SAIL FOR NORMANDY WITH 100 SHIPS.

PHILIP WAS LAYING SIEGE TO VERNEUIL CASTLE ON THE NORMANDY BORDER.

WHILE RICHARD WAS ON HIS WAY TO VERNEUIL, JOHN VISITED HIM.

DO NOT BE AFRAID, JOHN. YOU'VE FALLEN AMONG BAD COMPANY – THEY ARE THE MEN I WILL PUNISH.

AS RICHARD'S ARMY CLOSED ON VERNEUIL, PHILIP MADE A HASTY RETREAT.

JOHN'S ARMY IS NOW FIGHTING ON RICHARD'S SIDE, MY LORD.

RICHARD RETOOK CASTLE AFTER CASTLE. ON JULY 4, HE CAPTURED PHILIP'S SUPPLY WAGONS AND MUCH OF HIS TREASURE.

RICHARD REGAINED CONTROL OF AQUITAINE AND THE SOUTH. IN NORMANDY, THE STRUGGLE AGAINST PHILIP WENT ON FOR YEARS.

IN MID-1196, RICHARD DECIDED TO MAKE HIS MAIN BASE CAMP ON AN ISLAND IN THE SEINE RIVER. HE ORDERED THE SITE TO BE FORTIFIED AND NAMED IT CHÂTEAU-GAILLARD.

BY LATE 1198, RICHARD HAD GAINED THE UPPER HAND IN THE WAR. PHILIP NEARLY DROWNED WHILE FLEEING FROM RICHARD AND HIS MEN.

HELP ME! I'M SINKING!

ON MARCH 26, 1199, RICHARD WAS LAYING SIEGE TO A CASTLE IN LIMOUSIN. HE WAS NOT WEARING ARMOR WHEN HE WENT TO VIEW THE CASTLE DEFENSES...

WATCH OUT, MY LORD!

HA! A MISS!

GNNNG!

AARGH!

THE WOUND BECAME INFECTED.

SEND FOR MY MOTHER.

A FEW DAYS LATER...

I HAVE SEEN TOO MANY MEN IN THIS CONDITION. I KNOW THAT I WILL DIE.

HAVING FORGIVEN THE MAN WHO FIRED THE ARROW, KING RICHARD DIED ON APRIL 6, 1199.

THE END

GOOD KINGS & BAD

*O*n April 11, 1199, Richard's body was buried with his father's at the abbey church of Fontevraud in Touraine. He had spent most of his ten-year reign fighting in France and the Holy Land. His people had to raise a small fortune to free him from capture on his return. Yet the English remembered him as a hero – a great king, and a truly brave and chivalrous knight.

JOHN'S ACHIEVEMENTS
King John's reign saw many failures, but there were successes too. He improved the way tax was collected and recorded, as well as strengthening the power of England's law courts.

HEROES AND VILLAINS
Richard's brother inherited the Angevin Empire and was crowned King John I of England in London in May 1199. Unlike Richard, however, John was neither loved nor trusted by his people. Both brothers had fought their father and the king of France, as well as one another. But John's rebellions against Henry II, Richard, and Philip II of France were not forgotten. While Richard was to go down as one of the best kings in English history, John was to be remembered as one of the worst.

LOSSES IN FRANCE
John's reign was certainly a disaster for the Angevin Empire. One of his first acts after being crowned king of England was to settle a truce with Philip of France. It did not last long, however, and in 1202 the French king declared war against him. By 1206, Philip controlled all of John's northern lands, from Normandy to Touraine.

Innocent III played a major role in governments throughout Europe. He was one of the most powerful popes in history.

TROUBLE WITH THE POPE
In 1206, the quarrel also began with Pope Innocent III, the leader of the Christian church in Western Europe.

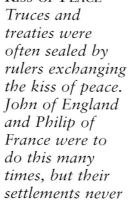

KISS OF PEACE
Truces and treaties were often sealed by rulers exchanging the kiss of peace. John of England and Philip of France were to do this many times, but their settlements never lasted long.

The argument was over who should be archbishop of Canterbury, the head of the English church. When John refused to accept Innocent's choice, the Pope banned church services in England. John did not give in to the Pope until 1213.

TROUBLE WITH THE NOBLES
John's English nobles were deeply unhappy with his activities at home and abroad. After Philip won a major victory in northern France in 1214, John's nobles rose against his rule. They forced him to agree to the Magna Carta. This document limited the king's power and gave more rights and power to the nobles. It also said that the country should be ruled by law and not by the king's will. John signed the Magna Carta on June 15, 1215. He died just over a year later.

THE FALL OF CHÂTEAU-GAILLARD
Richard's great fort of Château-Gaillard was captured by Philip's army in April 1204. Soon afterward, the French king was in control of all Normandy.

THE PEOPLE'S RIGHTS
Although the Magna Carta gave power to the English nobility, it did little for the ordinary people. In later years, however, it came to stand for the right of everyone to freedom and justice.

GLOSSARY

ally A person or group that supports another person or group.

banner A king or knight's streamerlike flag.

betray Being disloyal to someone or doing something to hurt him or her.

bombardment A fierce attack.

catapult A weapon used to toss large rocks or fire giant arrows.

chainmail Armor made from small metal rings linked together.

disguise To hide something.

fortify To strengthen a building or place against attack.

heir The person who receives possessions when the owner dies.

homage In the homage ceremony, a person knelt and swore to be loyal to his lord and to fight for him in times of war.

inherit To receive possessions after the owner's death.

invade To enter a region by force.

loyal Staying faithful and true to a person or a belief.

mercenary A soldier who serves in a foreign army and who fights for money or just for the love of war.

Muslim A follower of the religion of Islam, first preached by the prophet Muhammad in the 600s. Muslims believe that there is one God. Their holy book is called the Koran.

oath A solemn promise.

peasant Under feudalism, people who worked the land but did not own it. Peasants had few rights and were almost completely at the mercy of their lords.

pompous When someone thinks of themselves as being very important.

ransom Money paid in return for freeing a kidnapped person.

rear guard The soldiers who protect the rear of an army.

rebellion When people rise up against their leader or ruler.

revenge Action you take to pay someone back for harm that person has done to you.

rumor Something said by many people although it may not be true.

sermon A speech given during a religious service.

siege Surrounding a town or castle and cutting off its supplies, to force its people to give in.

slaughter The cruel killing of a large number of people.

squire A young man who served a knight and who was training to be a knight himself.

tournament Games in which knights fought each other on horseback.

FOR MORE INFORMATION

ORGANIZATIONS

Arizona Center for Medieval and Renaissance Studies
Arizona State University
P.O. Box 872301
Tempe, AZ 85287-2301
(480) 965-5900
Web site: http://www.asu.edu/clas/acmrs/index.html

The Metropolitan Museum of Art
1000 Fifth Avenue
New York, NY 10028-0198
(212) 535-7710
Web site: http://www.metmuseum.org/

FOR FURTHER READING

Cadnum, Michael. *The Book of the Lion*. New York: Penguin Putnam Books for Young Readers, 2001.

Doherty, Katherine M., and Craig A. Doherty. *King Richard the Lionhearted and the Crusades in World History*. Berkeley Heights, NJ: Enslow Publishers, Inc., 2002.

Hancock, Lee. *Saladin and the Kingdom of Jerusalem: The Muslims Recapture the Holy Land in AD 1187*. New York: The Rosen Publishing Group, Inc., 2004.

Hilliam, David. *Richard the Lionhearted and the Third Crusade: The English King Confronts Saladin, AD 1191*. New York: The Rosen Publishing Group, Inc., 2004.

Stalcup, Brenda. *The Crusades*. Farmington Hills, MI: Gale Group, 2000.

INDEX

Web Sites

Due to the changing nature of Internet links, the Rosen Publishing Group, Inc., has developed an online list of Web sites related to the subject of this book. This site is updated regularly. Please use this link to access the list:

http://www.rosenlinks.com/gnf/richard